American Symbols

The Liberty Bell

By Lloyd G. Douglas

Children's Press®
A Division of Scholastic Inc.
New York / Toronto / London / Auckland / Sydney
Mexico City / New Delhi / Hong Kong
Danbury, Connecticut

Photo Credits: Cover © Leif Skoogfors/Corbis; p. 5 © Lester Lefkowitz/Corbis; pp. 7, 17 © Bettmann/Corbis; p. 9 © National Archive and Records Administration; p. 11 © Bequest of Mrs. Benjamin Ogle/Corbis; p. 13 © Ed Eckstein/Corbis; p. 15 © Hulton Archive/Getty Images; p. 19 © H. Armstrong Roberts; p. 21 © Bob Krist/Corbis
Contributing Editor: Jennifer Silate
Book Design: Christopher Logan

Library of Congress Cataloging-in-Publication Data

Douglas, Lloyd G.
    The Liberty Bell / by Lloyd G. Douglas.
    p. cm.—(American symbols)
    Includes index.
    Summary: Uses easy-to-read text to introduce the Liberty Bell as an
    American symbol.
    ISBN 0-516-25852-4 (lib. bdg.)—ISBN 0-516-27875-4 (pbk.)
    1. Liberty Bell—Juvenile literature. 2. Philadelphia
    (Pa.)—Buildings, structures, etc.—Juvenile literature. [1. Liberty
    Bell. 2. Philadelphia (Pa.)—Buildings, structures, etc.] I. Title.

F158.8.I3D68 2003
974.8'11—dc21

                                        2002156198

Contents

1 American Symbol   4

2 A Crack in the Bell   12

3 Visiting the Liberty Bell   20

4 New Words   22

5 To Find Out More   23

6 Index   24

7 About the Author   24

The **Liberty** Bell is an American **symbol**.

It is a symbol of **freedom** in America.

PASS AND STOW
PHILADA
MDCCLIII

5

The Liberty Bell was made in 1752.

It was made to **celebrate** the **constitution** of Pennsylvania.

The FRAME of the

GOVERNMENT

OF THE

Province of Pennſilvania

IN

AMERICA:

Together with certain

LAWS

Agreed upon in England

BY THE

GOVERNOUR

AND

Divers FREE-MEN of the aforeſaid
PROVINCE.

To be further Explained and Confirmed there by the firſt
Provincial Council and General Aſſembly that ſhall
be held, if they ſee meet.

Printed in the Year MDCLXXXII.

FAC-SIMILE OF TITLE PAGE OF PENN'S "FRAME OF GOVERNMENT, 1682."

7

The Liberty Bell was **rung** many times.

In 1776, it was rung to celebrate the **Declaration of Independence**.

In CONGRESS, July 4, 1776.

The unanimous Declaration of the thirteen united States of America.

The last time the Liberty Bell rang was in 1846.

It was rung for George Washington's birthday.

11

The Liberty Bell has a big **crack** in it.

It does not ring anymore.

13

The Liberty Bell has been taken around the country.

Many people have seen it.

15

An American space ship was named after the Liberty Bell.

LIBERTY
BELL
7

17

A picture of the Liberty Bell is on a **coin**.

19

Many people visit the Liberty Bell each year.

It is an important American symbol.

21

New Words

celebrate (**sel**-uh-brate) to do something fun on a special occasion

coin (**koin**) a piece of metal with a picture and a number on it that is used as money

constitution (kon-stuh-**too**-shuhn) the system of laws in a country or state that tells the rights of the people and the powers of the government

crack (**krak**) a very thin break in something

Declaration of Independence (dek-luh-**ray**-shuhn **uhv** in-di-**pen**-duhnss) a document declaring the freedom of the thirteen American colonies from British rule

freedom (**free**-duhm) being able to go where you want or do what you want

liberty (**lib**-ur-tee) freedom

rung (**ruhng**) having made a clear musical sound

symbol (**sim**-buhl) a drawing or an object that stands for something else

To Find Out More

Books

The Liberty Bell
by Tristan Boyer Binns
Heinemann Library

The Liberty Bell: The Sounds of Freedom
by Jon Wilson
Child's World

Web Site

A to Z Kid's Stuff: Symbols of the USA
http://www.atozkidsstuff.com/symbols.html
Read facts and print a picture of the Liberty Bell and other American symbols to color on this Web site.

Index

celebrate, 6, 8
coin, 18
constitution, 6
crack, 12

Declaration of
  Independence, 8

freedom, 4

Pennsylvania, 6

space ship, 16
symbol, 4, 20

Washington,
  George, 10

About the Author
Lloyd G. Douglas is an editor and writer of children's books.

Reading Consultants
Kris Flynn, Coordinator, Small School District Literacy, The San Diego County
    Office of Education

Shelly Forys, Certified Reading Recovery Specialist, W.J. Zahnow Elementary
    School, Waterloo, IL

Sue McAdams, Former President of the North Texas Reading Council of the
    IRA, and Early Literacy Consultant, Dallas, TX